To: _____

From: _____

Date: _____

A mother is the truest
friend we have.
Washington Irving

Sweet Treats for Mom

Artwork by Lisa Kaus

HARVEST HOUSE PUBLISHERS

EUGENE, OREGON

Sweet Treats for Mom

Artwork Copyright © 2012 by Lisa Kaus

Published by Harvest House Publishers
Eugene, Oregon 97402
www.harvesthousepublishers.com

ISBN 978-0-7369-4606-3

All works of art reproduced in this book are copyrighted by Lisa Kaus and may not be reproduced without the artist's permission. For more information regarding art prints featured in this book, please contact:

Courtney Davis, Inc.
340 Main Street
Franklin, Tennessee 37064
www.courtneydavis.com

Design and production by Mary pat Design, Westport, Connecticut

Harvest House Publishers has made every effort to trace the ownership of all poems and quotes. In the event of a question arising from the use of a poem or quote, we regret any error made and will be pleased to make the necessary correction in future editions of this book.

All Scripture quotations, unless otherwise indicated, are taken from The Holy Bible, *New International Version®* NIV®. Copyright © 1973, 1978, 1984, 2011 by Biblica, Inc.™ Used by permission. All rights reserved worldwide.

Printed in China

13 14 15 16 17 18 / LP / 10 9 8 7 6 5 4 3 2

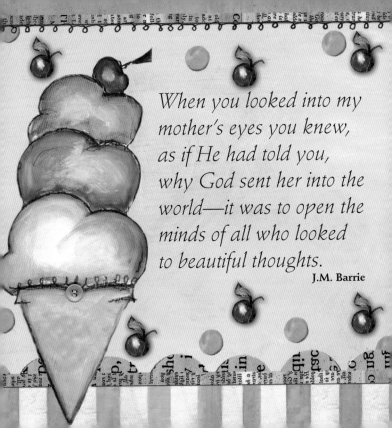

When you looked into my mother's eyes you knew, as if He had told you, why God sent her into the world—it was to open the minds of all who looked to beautiful thoughts.

J.M. Barrie

I celebrate you today!

Most of all the other beautiful things in life come by twos and threes, by dozens and hundreds —plenty of roses, stars, sunsets, rainbows, brothers and sisters, aunts and cousins—but only one mother in all the wide world.

Kate Douglas Wiggin

A mother is a mother, still the holiest thing alive.

Samuel Taylor Coleridge

Chocolate Pretzels

- ◆ Circular pretzels
- ◆ Milk chocolate buttons
- ◆ Candy-coated chocolate pieces

Place pretzels on baking sheet. Set one chocolate button in the center of each pretzel. Bake in preheated 350 degree oven for 1 to 2 minutes or until buttons melt. Remove from oven and press one candy-coated chocolate piece in the center of each pretzel. Chill until set.

SWEET TREATS TO TOP A CAKE:

- ❖ powdered sugar or cocoa dusted over doilies or stencils onto unfrosted cake
- ❖ buttercream frosting, thinly sliced oranges, fresh berries
- ❖ whipped cream, chocolate chips, and sprinkles

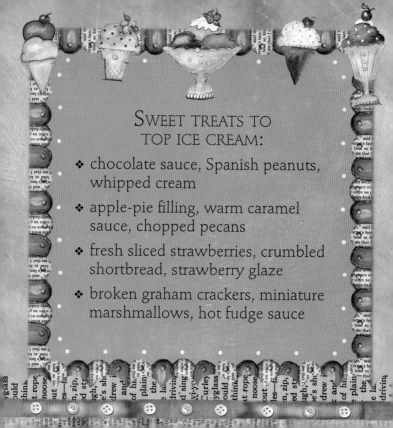

SWEET TREATS TO TOP ICE CREAM:

- ❖ chocolate sauce, Spanish peanuts, whipped cream
- ❖ apple-pie filling, warm caramel sauce, chopped pecans
- ❖ fresh sliced strawberries, crumbled shortbread, strawberry glaze
- ❖ broken graham crackers, miniature marshmallows, hot fudge sauce

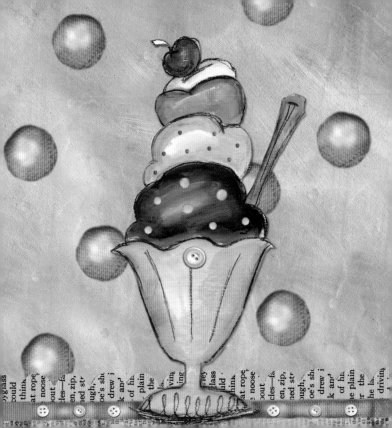

*Life began with waking up
and loving my mother's face.*

George Eliot

Mom, you sprinkle my world with happiness and layer my life with love. Your smiles fill my heart with joy.

Who ran to help me
when I fell,
And would some pretty
story tell,
Or kiss the place to
make it well?
My mother.

Ann Taylor

SWEET TREATS TO WARM
A MOM'S HEART:

- ❖ her baby's smile
- ❖ her husband's love
- ❖ her Lord's blessing

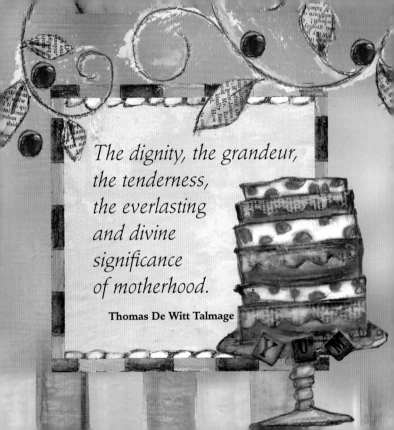

The dignity, the grandeur, the tenderness, the everlasting and divine significance of motherhood.

Thomas De Witt Talmage

Piled high with fluffy pink frosting, here's a cupcake for you and a cupcake for me. Let's party!

The mother's heart is the child's schoolroom.

Henry Ward Beecher

Pineapple Cream Cheese Frosting/Pudding

- 1 (3.4 ounce) package instant vanilla pudding mix
- 1 cup milk
- 1 (8 ounce) package cream cheese, softened
- 1 (8 ounce) container frozen whipped topping, thawed
- 1 (15 ounce) can crushed pineapple, drained

Mix the vanilla pudding mix with the milk. Blend in the cream cheese. Fold in the frozen whipped topping and crushed pineapple. Frost a white or yellow cake or enjoy as a pudding.

*A mother understands
what a child does not say.*

Jewish Proverb

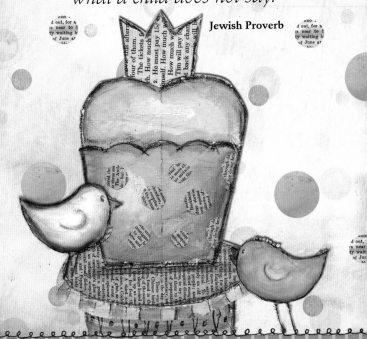

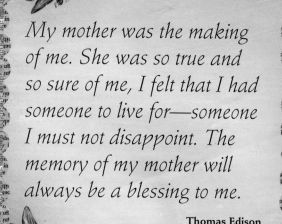

My mother was the making of me. She was so true and so sure of me, I felt that I had someone to live for—someone I must not disappoint. The memory of my mother will always be a blessing to me.

Thomas Edison

Sweater, n.: garment worn by child when its mother is feeling chilly.

Ambrose Bierce

SWEET TREATS TO FIX A BAD DAY:

- ❖ a candlelit bubble bath
- ❖ time with a good book
- ❖ decadent chocolate truffles

SWEET TREATS TO START A PERFECT DAY:

- ❖ delicious cream scones
- ❖ hot brewed tea
- ❖ time with God

Mother is the name for God in the lips and hearts of little children.

William Makepeace Thackeray

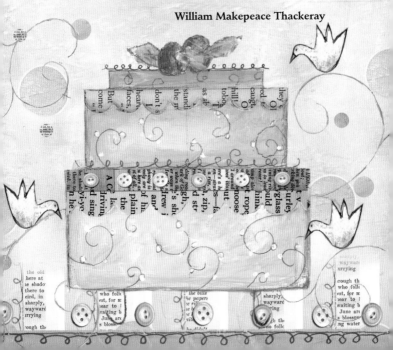

eat

CAKE

The best academy—a
mother's knee.

James Russell Lowell

SWEET TREATS TO
REVIVE A WEARY MOM:

❖ fluffy down pillows

❖ Grandma's quilt

❖ an afternoon nap and sweet dreams

LETS EAT CAKE

Peanut Butter Popcorn

- 2 (3.5 ounce) bags microwave popcorn
- 1/2 cup margarine
- 3/4 cup brown sugar
- 1/4 cup peanut butter
- 20 large marshmallows

Microwave the popcorn and pour into a large bowl. In a separate glass bowl, combine margarine, brown sugar, and marshmallows. Cook for 1 minute in microwave on high. Stir and repeat until mixture is melted and smooth. Add the peanut butter and mix until well blended. Pour mixture over popcorn and stir quickly to coat well.

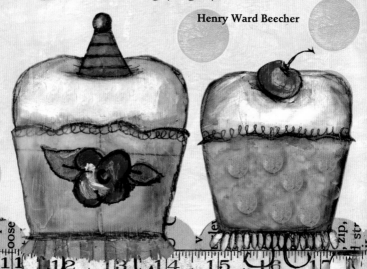

God pardons like a mother who kisses the offense into everlasting forgetfulness.

Henry Ward Beecher

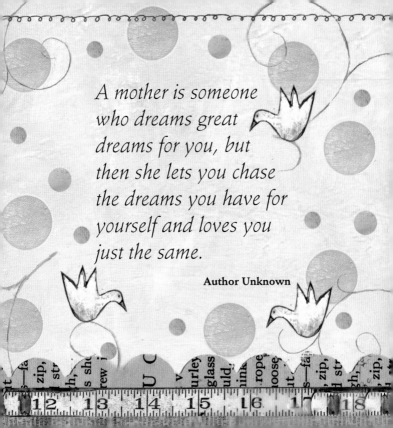

A mother is someone who dreams great dreams for you, but then she lets you chase the dreams you have for yourself and loves you just the same.

Author Unknown

Sweets to the sweet.

William Shakespeare

SWEET TREATS TO TOP A
CELEBRATION:

❖ a gathering of friends

❖ big, bright bouquets of flowers

❖ making lifetime memories

SWEET TREATS FOR A RAINY AFTERNOON:

❖ steaming hot cocoa

❖ warm buttery popcorn

❖ a favorite movie

Peaches and Cream

- 1 large peach
- 1 teaspoon brown sugar
- 2 tablespoons sour cream
- 1 tablespoon pecans, chopped

Peel, pit, and slice the peach. Sprinkle
it with the brown sugar, sour cream,
and chopped pecans. Serve chilled.

You've covered me in love—
warm hugs and sweet
kisses—my whole life long.
I love you so much.

SWEET TREATS A MOM LOVES TO HEAR:

- ❖ songbirds in the morning
- ❖ children's laughter
- ❖ the words "I love you"

SWEET TREATS TO
BREATHE IN DEEPLY:

- ❖ fresh baked bread
- ❖ a bouquet of lilacs
- ❖ vanilla candles

I remember my mother's prayers, and they have always followed me. They have clung to me all of my life.

Abraham Lincoln

The tie which links
mother and child is
of such pure and
immaculate strength
as to be never
violated.

Washington Irving

The sweet stuff in life matters: dense chocolate cake, yummy butter frosting, sprinkles that sparkle, and frosty cold ice cream.

Chocolate-Dipped Strawberries

- 1 pound fresh strawberries
- 16 ounces milk chocolate chips
- 2 tablespoons shortening
- wooden toothpicks

Insert toothpick into top of each strawberry. In a double boiler, melt the chocolate chips and shortening, stirring constantly until smooth. Use toothpicks to dip strawberries into the chocolate mixture. Stick toothpicks into Styrofoam block, allowing the chocolate-dipped strawberries to cool before serving.

*Grace comes into the soul,
as the morning sun into
the world; first a dawning;
then a light; and at last
the sun in his full and
excellent brightness.*

Thomas Adams

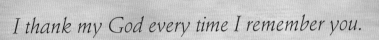

I thank my God every time I remember you.

The Book of Philippians

Thank you for loving me,
Mom. I am blessed.

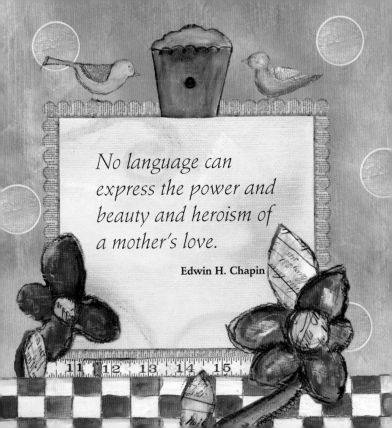

No language can express the power and beauty and heroism of a mother's love.

Edwin H. Chapin

She is clothed with strength and
    dignity; she can laugh at the days
    to come.
She speaks with wisdom, and faithful
    instruction is on her tongue.
She watches over the affairs of her
    household and does not eat the
    bread of idleness.
Her children arise and call her
    blessed.

The Book of Proverbs

Oh the experience of this sweet life. **Dante**

Apple Delight

- 2 (21 ounce) cans apple pie filling
- 1 (18.25 ounce) package yellow cake mix
- 1/2 cup butter, melted

Preheat oven to 350 degrees. Pour apple pie filling into a 9x13-inch pan. Sprinkle cake mix over pie filling. Drizzle melted butter on top, stir slightly to evenly moisten dry cake batter. Bake 30 minutes. Serve hot or cold.

Beautiful as seemed mama's face, it became more lovely when she smiled and seemed to enliven everything about her.

Leo Tolstoy

Sugar and spice
whip up nice!

Today let's eat cake. Let's eat cake every day!

SWEET TREATS TO TOP
OFF A GOOD DAY:

- ❖ pink sunsets
- ❖ fireflies
- ❖ shooting stars

A happy family is but an earlier heaven.

Sir John Bowering

SWEET TREATS TO
REFRESH A MOM'S SOUL:

❖ a gentle breeze

❖ words of encouragement

❖ a walk on a sunny seashore

Thank you for being
my mom *and* my friend.
You flavor my world with love.